WRITING A NONPROFIT GRANT PROPOSAL

A GUIDE IN WRITING WINNING PROPOSALS
THAT WILL HELP YOU GET FUNDS
FOR YOUR PLANS AND PROJECTS

FRANK COLES

Table of Contents

INTRODUCTION

Grant writing is an art, and many talented grant writers hone their skills over several years. Organizations hire these writers, and their sole responsibility is to submit grant proposals. However, your organization may not be in the position to hire a grant writer at this moment. Lucky for you, grant writing is an art, and art is something you can learn.

As Malcolm Gladwell writes in his book Outliers: The Story of Success. All it takes to become an expert is a whole lot of practice. Gladwell suggests that you need to practice for 10,000 hours, roughly 20 hours a week, for ten years to become an expert in anything. Some feel that 10,000 hours is impossible, but on the other hand, Gladwell reminds me that anything I want to master is possible with a little (or a lot) of practice.

Grant writing is no different. Those interested in learning how to write grants learn a little and then practice by writing a proposal or two. Afterwards, they learn from their successes or mistakes, and then they move on to the next grant proposal.

Grant funding helps organizations and individuals to achieve their goals. Grants are a way to acquire funds and stretch organizational capacities. Nonprofits use grants to feed children, provide workforce development, and offer housing to individuals living in poverty. Businesses use grants to launch new and innovative ideas as well as create more substantial infrastructures. Individuals receive grant funds; they use these awards to support research, create art, or for education. Grant funding makes impossible goals possible; therefore, learning how to write successful proposals is not only helpful, but it can also be fun.

Still, I should mention that grant writing is not a quick fix; it is a long process of research and relationship-building. The benefits of grant writing surpass that of just the funds awarded. The grant-seeking process helps you to build relationships with external stakeholders who will support your cause. In many ways, these relationships are as valuable as the awarded funds because they instill trust. They offer you an opportunity to prove your project's worth, and they leverage future funding with other grantors.

The grant writing process may seem confusing and overwhelming; the purpose of this book is to help you to feel more confident in your ability to write successful proposals. You have a project that is going to change the world for the better, and I want to give you as many tools as I can to help you achieve your goals.

What is a Grant?

Grants are money awarded from an organization to an individual, business, or nonprofit for a specific purpose. They are a strategic collaboration between two entities to make a positive change in the world. To be awarded grant money, an applicant must request the funds through a detailed process. It is unlikely that a grantor will send money to an organization or individual who hasn't formally applied. Even more so that money given is without specific restrictions and requirements.

There are different ways for organizations to fund activities. Businesses rely mostly on the earned income of sales, non-profits raise funds through donations and applying for grants, and individuals either sell items or receive money from supporters through gifts. Additionally, all groups can apply for grants to fund projects.

Who can Apply for a Grant?

The truth is that an overwhelming majority of grants are awarded to nonprofit organizations but it doesn't mean that grants are only designed for nonprofit organizations; many businesses and individuals receive grant funds.

Nonprofit Organizations

Grants are designed to fund organizations and individuals to help the society, which makes nonprofits a good choice. This is the reason why many grantors are likely to support nonprofit organizations.

Businesses

Businessmen or entrepreneurs often ask, "Where can I find for-profit grant opportunities?" For-profit business grants are somewhat difficult to find than grant opportunities for nonprofits, but they do exist.

Federal agencies such as grant opportunities from the U.S. Small Business Administration and the Department of Agriculture and corporate foundations like the FedEx Small Business Grant Contest are examples of opportunities that are available to businesses.

When researching and applying for business grants, it is best to consider what makes your organization stand out. Are you a female business owner or a veteran, disabled, or Native American? If so, there are specific grant opportunities available for you. Is your business a start-up or a tech company? There are fewer grant opportunities for large established corporations, but you open your company up to possibilities if you are a small, native-owned business.

Typical business grants (and loans) would require a current business plan. Business plans should outline the current goals, objectives of the business, and funding requirements.

Individuals

If you are an individual looking to buy a home or receive emergency assistance, you probably won't find much luck with grants. However, you can look to your local social service agencies for that type of support. The grants available for individuals tend to fall under three categories: Academic Research, Scholarships, Art Fellowships. If your project falls under those three categories, you should find opportunities from different social service agencies.

Fiscal Agents: Sometimes, it is easier for individuals to receive grant funds if they have a fiscal sponsor. Financial sponsors or organizations that will manage the funds for the individual and that allow the individual to apply for grants primarily as a program of the organizations. You may want to consider partnering with a fiscal agent if you are having trouble securing grants as an individual.

Consider Options: Another aspect to consider is whether your project is best suited for incorporation as a business or a non-profit. There are more grant opportunities for organizations, so you may want to bite the bullet and set up a formal structure like a business or a nonprofit to accomplish your project goals. Speak with a consultant or check out your state's Licensing and Regulatory Agency to establish an entity

LAYING THE GROUNDWORK

Grant Proposal's Need Statement vs. Business Plan's Research & Analysis

In grant proposals, nonprofit agencies usually begin with a declaration of needs that illustrate the problems faced by clients or society, the extent of the obstacles, and its complexity. In the same way, business plans address consumers' needs in the market research chapters, which provide an overview of the consumer, the marketplace (also called the social sector environment), and competition. In this step of business preparation, the companies must explain the anticipated demand for their planned good or service (e.g., market size) and present the marketplace and the competitive conditions that will influence the performance (e.g., advantageous or unfavorable circumstances) of the project.

Nonprofit Classification

Nonprofits became common in the United States. But people rarely know how different nonprofit organizations are established, identified by the IRS, or what they're doing. If you're unsure about nonprofit organizations and how they vary from nonprofit institutions, don't feel guilty. We prefer to pile all nonprofits into one stack, although there are many forms of nonprofits.

It is essential to consider the category of a nonprofit that you are part of and the federal rules and standards that your company is supposed to comply with. When investigating grant funds, it is necessary to test and see what kinds of nonprofits a specific funder is providing grants to. Research is the key.

The federal government has given a nonprofit corporation tax-exempt to the central government. Nonprofit entities are governed by the federal government and must comply with particular laws, legislation, and management procedures. In the United States, the Internal Revenue Service bears the responsibility of controlling the corporate activities of non-profit organizations. At the state level, nonprofit corporations are expected to hold all non-profit or fundraising licenses and submit all Articles of Incorporation.

Nonprofit Regulation

A nonprofit corporation has been given tax-exempt status by the federal government. Non-profit Many grants, including those provided by federal and state governments, allow each non-profit to have a DUNS number while applying for a grant. DUNS stands for Data Universal Numbering System, established by the credit processing firm Dun and Bradstreet in 1962. The procurement of a DUNS number is free of charge and ensures the funder that the non-profit in question is fiscally responsible.

Acquiring a DUNS Number

Many grants, including those provided by federal and state governments, allow each non-profit to have a DUNS number while applying for a grant. DUNS stands for Data Universal Numbering System, established by the credit processing firm Dun and Bradstreet in 1962. The procurement of a DUNS number is free of charge and ensures the funder that the nonprofit in question is fiscally responsible.

Grant Availability Research

Studying where and what kinds of grants is a time-consuming and energy-wasting phase in the grant writing process. As a guideline, it is best to seek funding locally and use local grant funds effectively before pursuing state or federal grants. In comparison, it is tempting to apply for state and federal funding right off the bat because the grant awards are much more significant and more far-reaching. These funders like to see that you have a good record with a local grantor before considering a substantial grant from your nonprofit organization.

For some organizations, such as schools and hospitals, this may not apply, but smaller nonprofit organizations must first establish themselves as a basic rule. When seeking grants, you should find grantors that are a perfect fit for your company. Every foundation and giving organization has a set of grant criteria that typically spell out what type of projects and services they can donate money to.

The internet is a source of knowledge about the foundations and companies that award grants. The Foundations Center (foundationcenter) is a reliable starting tool. This website provides commercial and subsidized grant search engines at the city, national, federal, and corporate levels. It's a safe place to start preparing for potential grants.

Making Contacts

Communication with prospective funders is one of the most critical facets of the grant-seeking process. Unfortunately, that may also make sure people experience the most disturbing aspect since we don't want to hear the word "no." However, having a friendly "no" early in the process can save you lots of time and energy, making sure that your grant writing becomes more productive and successful. Again, its best, to begin with the local foundations and companies, many of which are community organizations.

Get acquainted with local organizations, spend time networking on board members, and make business ties. Private outreach is the best – people want to have a personal attachment to a grant application. Spending your time at local non-profit forums and gatherings is a perfect place to promote your non-profit, talk about your project, and catch up with potential funders face to face. Most of the foundations and funding companies have a grant administrator or an officer in charge of the applications. You should ask this representative by phone about the support you are applying for and find out what the foundation has to give.

Now, you're ready to begin the process of drafting the grant application.

STEPS IN DEVELOPING A GRANT PROPOSAL

Planning Begins at Home

Before you can realize the optimal approach for getting grant funds for your small business, you must first be very clear about your business. What is the mission of your endeavor?

The bottom line is: You've got to know what your business is all about. You may *think* you know your business and that you're ready to dive right into getting money to support it. In truth, though, every new business owner has much to learn from business planning. It's not easy to get started with a business plan, but you'll find the activity gratifying and even essential once you get rolling.

Business planning is an exercise that can help you connect with the core mission of your business. It's just as much a philosophical and reflexive activity as it is a logistical and financial one. Many companies and organizations, even those already fully developed, delegate a certain period and a specific delegation of person-hours every year to develop business plans.

From start-ups to blue chips, creating business plans can help you build your company's identity and culture while helping to generate powerful and innovative ideas. Thus, the culmination of your business planning efforts will make your ultimate grant proposal that much more informed and thereby more powerful.

Do yourself massive favor from the get-go. Set aside a week or month (depending on the scale of your business endeavor) to **PLAN**. Your *Executive Summary* will clarify your business' purpose and help you get a better idea of which granting organizations would be most receptive to your petitions. The content you create for your Executive Summary will also be beneficial to the *Need Statement* that you will soon author at the beginning of your grant proposal writing process.

Your *Financial Statements* or *Proposal Budget* will help you clarify how much money you will need to acquire from grant funding. Remember, your funding sources should be diverse between grants, personal funds, venture capital, and other investors, etc.

Once you have a solid business plan (or at very least a tremendous Executive Summary and clear Financial Statements), you're ready to start scouting grant-giving organizations.

Finding the Perfect Grantor

Though there are 26 federal grant-making agencies, if you're not a non-profit organization, you're not going to get a grant from the federal government unless your business focuses on research and development or environmental stewardship. Your business may qualify for the SBIR program (Small Business Innovation Research).

The SBIR program focuses on helping small companies to develop and market technologically innovative products.

If your business falls in a gray area and you're not sure whether you qualify for federal funding, then check the Catalog of Federal Domestic Assistance (CFDA). The CFDA is a database containing all of the federal programs available to organizations and individuals. You will have to sift through a lot of white noise — programs well outside the scope of your endeavor— but hey, no one said this was going to be an easy process.

State and local governments, as well as non-profit programs, do offer grants to small businesses. Usually, these programs will ask that the grant be matched with another funding source, such as a loan or personal investment. To explore these local opportunities, go to the government websites for your state and local governments, or contact your state senator or representative.

Here are a few foundation/private organizations that offer small business grants:

Amber Grant – The Amber Foundation Grant focuses on helping women achieve in business. It was started in 1998 and did not award vast sums of money, but a modest $500-$1000 to help driven women — pursuing a traditional or online business — get up and running.

Business Owners IdeaCafe Small Business Grant – This grant is all about whose idea is the most creative. The grant is awarded to an innovative business that will receive $1000 in cash and a $500 advertising credit.

Intuit Love Our Local Business – The technology company, Intuit, the brains behind TurboTax and Mint, have made the grant-award process democratic with their *Love Our Local Business* grant. Customers, employees, and vendors can nominate companies they find deserving, and the winners receive a few thousand dollars from playing. Since its inception, the *Love Our Local Business* grant has awarded 1.1 million dollars.

Grant opportunities can be challenging to find, so if you're going to take the time and trouble, the application you submit should be nothing short of excellent.

As far as this grand-finding research phase goes, I highly recommend using your day-planner or calendar app to pencil in 2-3 hours per day for several weeks to for your grant-hunting efforts. That will help you to avoid being overwhelmed or burning out.

Crafting the Statement of Need

You're going to need to pay very close attention to the forms you receive, which dictate how your grant proposal is structured. Some grant-giving organizations will simply choose to discard a plan that isn't correctly formatted. You will also want to echo back the verbiage and style used by the grant-giving organization. Often the grant paperwork will spell out the purposes and objectives of the grant-giving organization. If you can mirror these purposes and goals, you're more likely to have the grant awarded to your small business.

Since you may be applying to obtain more than one grant, I recommend that you write one "generic" application just so that you have a consistent baseline to work from. And that you have fully wrapped your head around what is it that you need and why your business deserves it. Then be sure to take time to mold it to the specific requirements of each application when the time comes.

Before diving into any specific Grant Application, you need to get the application guidelines and deadlines. You'll also want to find a contact person you can reach out to if you have any questions about specific Grant Application requirements. Most Grant Applications you'll see begins with a Need Statement.

The Need Statement is essentially the Executive Summary of your grant application and is the first step in writing out your grant proposal. As the name implies, this is where you articulate the need your business or organization has for funding. It's essential that the Need Statement closely aligns with the interest of the grant-awarding organization. In addition to expressing what your business needs financially, you should try to align it with whatever world-wide or community need your business aims to help fulfill.

Your Need Statement should bring to light, qualify, and quantify a specific problem. Your Need Statement should begin with assessing the scale of the problem – where is the problem, how rampant, vast, widespread – and the cause of the problem.

Here are some other steps you can take to ensure that your Need Statement is in pique condition.

- Make sure it's concise: If you're a small business owner, you probably have a lot of inside knowledge and know-how about your industry. When writing your Needs Statement, you need to leave the "shop talk" and industry jargon at home to relate to a lay audience. Keep it nice and simple, clear, and straightforward. Have a few of your friends (who aren't involved in your specific industry) read it to make sure it flows nicely and is easy to understand by an "outsider."

- Use a mix of stories and data: Telling stories about why your small business should be awarded grant money can be an effective way to persuade but make sure that the stories you choose to tap into the grand giving organization's indigenous interests. Be sure to have clear and compelling data to support your accounts. For example, if you are proposing a new burn case facility, it's ok to tell the story of a local burn victim who is lacking adequate care. Still, you would also want to include statistics detailing the total number of burn victims residing in the area where you're proposing the new care facility.

- Focus on the service, not the Need: Even though it's called a Needs Statement, you should focus your attention on "who" is being served. Whether it's the need of the community, the environment, or a group of people, describe what your small business is doing (or needs to do) to be of service. Give a clear, simple description of how your Small Business addresses this need, and allow the "need" of funding for your business to be secondary. In the end, the demand for financing will be apparent. So in concept, you're telling the review committee, "The community desperately needs this particular service that my business can provide. Here are all the reasons why. (But hey, by the way, I can't do any of this without getting some money first.)"

- <u>Use Outside Sources, Facts, and Opinions:</u> Show that you've done your homework and are onto something important. State opinions from qualified experts and showcase the facts that surround your service endeavor. When you show statistics, make sure they're clear and uncluttered (eliminate redundant data) and make an ironclad point.

In a nutshell, your Need Statement is a very well stated and sophisticated human interest story, equal parts of pathos and logos.

Take some time to learn a bit more about persuasive narrative, also known as a persuasive copy or persuasive copywriting. Your Needs Statement must be nothing short of *gripping*. Think — your proposal will be read by someone who's likely trying to narrow the field down from a hundred or more plans. She is probably looking for reasons to pass up your project and thin the herd. Don't let her! Be confident that you can write persuasively.

Writing the Goals and Objectives for your Grant Proposal

Again, the theme of quality and quantity returns. Here, quality and quantity can be used to demonstrate the difference between Goals and Objectives. Most grant applications would require you to write a section on your business's Goals and Objectives. The difference between the two lay in the ability to quantify. For grant writing, you can quantify an objective, while goals are more intangible.

When describing your goals, you must again connect with the mission(s) of the grant-giving organization. It's also alright to be a little dramatic here and using language that's a bit more fancy and persuasive. You should probably keep the goals short and the objectives a little longer. Your objectives will require a slightly longer description. Make sure that the objectives you set for your business are reasonable and attainable. Don't go into process details during this section. You'll have plenty of time for that in other sections of the proposal.

The objectives you set forth should be the things that can be accomplished within the grant period. But, you should not specify how you will achieve these objectives in this section; instead, you should determine how you will measure these objectives. It is also important to consider any expense you'll incur to take these measurements.

WRITING THE GRANT PROPOSAL

A typical proposal has the following sections appearing roughly in the following order:

1. Title

2. Executive Summary (if applicable)

3. Overall Goal

4. Background and Rationale

5. Significance and Impact

6. Methodology

   o Objective 1

      ▪ Specific Aim 1

         ▪ Approach

         ▪ Preliminary Results (if any)

      ▪ Specific Aim 2

- Specific Aim *x*

- Expected Results

  o Objective 2

  o Objective *x*

7. Work Plan

8. Key Personnel

9. Budget

Depending on your discipline, there is likely to be some variation in the actual order coupled with minor inclusions and exclusions. Particular attention should be paid to specific formats required by funding agencies.

The order they appear as presented above is typically not the order you will write them in and that is okay. My perspective on the writing order and the rationale for the same follows. My proposed order would be:

1. Title

2. Overall Goal

3. Methodology

   o Objective 1

   - Specific Aim 1

     - Approach

     - Preliminary Results (if any)

- Specific Aim 2

- Specific Aim x

- Expected Results

o Objective 2

o Objective x

4. Background and Rationale

5. Significance and Impact

6. Work Plan

7. Executive Summary (if applicable)

8. Key Personnel

9. Budget

As we begin our discussion on the proposal writing process, I would refer you to the table that presents a quick reference for where the outline for these sections can be found within the log frame already developed. Why do I advocate this particular order?

The budget's position is the easiest to explain. It comes at the end of the proposal preparation process when you have discussed everything that you plan to do. The development of the budget provides estimates of the cost of carrying out the project. Anything you change in the central part of the proposal has an impact on your budget. That is why the budget is the last item to be completed.

Proposal		Logframe
Impact	←	Goals
Overall goals	←	Purpose
Objectives/Expected Results	←	Outputs
Specific Aims	←	Major Activities

Correspondence between the log frame elements (project design) and the proposal sections

The Overall Goal and Methodology are the first areas to be tackled. The Overall Goal states what you want to achieve. Until you have a clear indication of what you want to achieve, you cannot do anything else as it determines everything else.

From the completion of the overall goal, you begin next on the methodology. This section captures the Objectives and their corresponding Specific Aims and the Expected Results. Recall that the Overall Goal and the Objectives are derived from the log frame Purpose and the Outputs, respectively.

You have already done a lot of the background review as you were formulating your ideas. You have brought yourself up to date with the literature and established what has been done. You also have a good understanding of the fundamental problems currently present in the project area. That was the basis of developing the hierarchy-impacts diagram, the objectives tree, and the log frame. This information will be essential for developing the following two sections: Background and Rationale and Significance and Impact.

Your attention now turns to the background and the Rationale section. You should have a lot of notes in support of this section from the literature reviewed during the problem and project design. It is important to note that there is a big distinction between background and rationale. Background places your work in the context of what has been done and the situation on the ground.

The rationale is the reasoning behind why out of all the many problems that are out there. You have selected this particular problem to work on. Both should be placed in the context of the problems and linkages identified in the hierarchy-impacts diagram.

In the Significance and Impact section, the importance of the project must be clearly spelled out. This is where many grant proposals fail. If the funding agency does not see the significance or importance of what you are proposing, they will not fund it.

It is a very crucial section that should not be buried in another section. It should stand out with its heading. For example, when you write your CV, you want to highlight those significant aspects of your life that would enable you to get employment. You do this by having particular sections in the CV like: academic qualifications, work experience, and so on, each with a distinct heading. You do not bury or mix these key areas.

A potential employer who is looking for your work experience, for example, can go directly to that section. Similarly, in your proposal, a potential reviewer who wants to see the Significance and Impact of your proposed project should navigate that section directly.

You are now in a position to write the Executive Summary. By definition, an executive summary is a complete summary of the proposal. That is why it is done towards the end, as you cannot summarize what you have not written.

Coming up with an appropriate Title follows. The title is the first point of contact a proposal reviewer has with you. A reviewer will receive a batch of proposals, typically with a list of titles. At this initial point of contact with you, the reviewer begins to form an opinion on your proposal – whether you believe that this fair or unfair is not important.

Reviewers are humans, after all. Therefore, your title must be able to capture and convey what you are trying to do entirely. It should not be too long. Many funding agencies limit the number of words that can be in the title. Sometimes you want to say everything (read too much) in the title. Composing a title is mainly playing with words to develop a concise sentence, and adequately captures and conveys the message on what you plan to do.

The final three elements, the Work Plan, Key Personnel, and the Budget, are then completed in that order. Clearly state your central idea often. State it in your executive summary, in the specific aims, in the summaries at the end, in the methodology, etc. It ensures that you are continually reminding the reviewer of what you are proposing to do. Use relevant literature to build the case in support of your central ideas. You have to be very confident that you know the current state of the art in your discipline so that whatever you are proposing is building on what others have done. It is unlikely that your area has never been researched upon by anyone, anywhere, at any point in time.

Although, a checklist is not part of your proposal, you should have one. A list ensures that you have not forgotten anything. Many funding agencies have stringent requirements on how their plans should be written, what they should contain, and which additional documents must be attached.

You should put all those requirements on a checklist, checking off what you have completed, thus ensuring your proposal is not thrown out because you did not meet a particular need. It should be updated regularly each time the proposal writing team meets.

Please note that this section has provided a set of our guidelines, not rules cast in stone. Our brains work differently. You may find that your mind prefers to write the proposal sections in a different order. We will now look at each of these proposal sections in a little more detail.

SN	Section	Status	Resp.	Comments
1	**MANDATORY DOCUMENTS**			
1.1	Duly filled application form (pg. 87-88 of RFP)	DONE	MO	
1.2	Integrity declaration form (pg. 101 of RFP)	DONE	DJM	Signed
1.3	Certified copy of company registration	PENDING	FM	To be certified
1.4	Organization Profile	DONE	CW	
2	**PROPOSAL**			
2.1	**Preliminaries**			
2.1.1	Impacts-hierarchy diagram and objec-tives tree	DONE	DJM/MO	
2.1.2	Logframe	DONE	DJM/MO	First draft
2.2	**Main Document**			
2.2.1	Title/Executive Summary	PENDING	DJM/MO	
2.2.2	Overall Goal	DONE	DJM/MO	
2.2.3	Background and Rationale	PENDING	DJM/MO	
2.2.4	Significance and Impact	PENDING	DJM/MO	
2.2.5	Methodology	STARTED	DJM/MO	
2.2.6	Work plan	PENDING	CW	
2.2.7	Budget	PENDING	CW	
2.3	**Appendices**			
2.3.1	MO - CV	DONE	MO	
2.3.2	DJM - CV	DONE	DJM	
2.3.3	CW - CV	DONE	CV	
3	**FORMAT REQUIREMENTS**			
3.1	Maximum 25 pages. 12pt font. Times New Roman	ON GOING	CW	To monitor
4	**FUNDING GUIDELINES**			
4.1	Funding range: A$ 200-400,000	ON GOING	CW	To monitor
4.2	Project duration maximum 3 years	ON GOING	CW	To monitor
4.3	Co-funding? Can we include in-kind items?	ON GOING	MO	To monitor
4.4	Eligible costs only direct costs, com-munication, engagement and capacity building	ON GOING	DJM	To monitor

TIPS & TRICKS TO WRITING A WINNING GRANT PROPOSAL

Tip 1: Consider the Amount of Effort Involved In the Writing Process

Although, you're excited to make money for your new ventures, the squad does not lose sight of the shoreline. You must pay attention to the actual effort and hard work needed to plan an excellent grant application. For example, if the company devotes time and energy to cultivating opportunities and analysis to engaging significant contributors, the same degree of consistency is expected in the written grant. This is mostly to ensure that the plan is well-developed and that the set goals are achieved. Since grants represent a large sum of money for organizations that apply for them, it means that the entity that earns them needs to show that:

- The mission is worth spending time and in line with the granting body.

- The activity is sustainable.

- The programs and initiatives must work concerning the grant funds.

It is also crucial that you already have fully-formed ideas and goals that need to be funded. You must always keep in mind that there should be allotted time to draft the grant proposal and the submission of the application. Few grant programs require the delivery of the request firsthand before they consider the plan. You must add the following details to this letter:

- A basic illustration of the organizational structure.

- A comprehensive history and context details.

- An in-depth description of the model and plans of the system.

- The estimated budget

- Prospective collaborations

The fact that the grant application needs so many moving pieces is not necessarily a safe idea to compose it on its own. Take a look at the broader picture! The only way to achieve it is to collaborate with a cohesive team to ensure that each of the leaders know the whole project's complexity.

Tip 2: Don't Chase the Money

You've got to apply and qualify. "Make sure your purpose and goals fits well with the mission of the supporting body," experts say. We should learn the critical lesson in hindsight: "Just apply for grants that look like they're written especially for you or your company," someone says regarding applying for grants and getting turned down several times because they didn't suit their purpose.

Tip 3: Knowing the Funder Means You Can Tailor Your Proposal

One thing you should note during the drafting process is that grant writing begins with your specific project. It doesn't generally have to start with the grant that you like to obtain. If you look at stuff like that, the strategy would be successful in the long term. This is mainly because:

- Beginning with your mission forces you to develop plans and making them more valid.

- Characterizing your goals with simplicity helps you to identify a grant provider whose purpose is closely matched to yours.

These two will boost your chances of having a winning proposal. Also, the waste of resources will be minimized during the whole process. You will need to perform serious research to determine the appropriate grant to be applied for. Once you have recognized a particular grant that is compatible with your key interests, the next move is to explore the grant's origins.

It is also critical that you let your organization's integrity and dedication shine through the entire application. Do this by putting forward the ideas that need funding to get the stakeholders on the initiative. This will reveal opportunities that are unique, significant, and meaningful. This will now serve as an excellent point of discussion in your grant proposal.

Tip 4: Look at Who and What Had Been Financed Before

Grant programs usually list the previous recipients of the award in their websites. If not, the institution's grant office may give you a list of persons on your place who have received the same grants you are seeking. This list is essential because it demonstrates the agency's interest in funding that kind of body.

Funders could also provide an internet-based list of former and existing grant reviewers and their affiliates. Check the list and ask yourself whether their expertise overlaps with the objectives and methodology of your proposal. It will be a high-risk idea to submit a grant for a fund that has never supported an initiative in your field of expertise before.

The broader picture is for you to understand the mission and the objectives of the program, and then look for opportunities that coincide with them. The tactic is not to formulate your proposal in line with the grant requirements. Instead, tailoring the proposal to ensure that the specific concept is by the grant criteria.

Tip 5: Don't Worry About Being Personal When Writing A Grant Proposal

Relationships are relevant to the world of nonprofit organizations. Linkages with the organization, its members, the population, the governments, and the electoral districts are essential to your progress. This is true in the case of grant writing, mainly if the grant-giving system is locally focused. One of the effective methods to get in touch is when you ask for more information or further discuss the criteria. But never slip into the pit of calling the grant agent just to make an impression.

Some grant programs require applicants not to message the grant officer, so make sure that you first check before any move is made. The wider picture is to approach a grant officer or someone else who knows about this to give you a glimpse into what the funding system is looking for. Do this only if it isn't expressly prohibited. This would not only help to guide the writing process but will also make a major difference.

Writing a grant proposal is specifically serious for nonprofit organizations. It means that you should do it with meticulous preparation, trust in the ideals of what you do, and reasonable hopes of creating a successful grant application. It would also require a specific way of thinking that you have so much to learn in the process.

DRAFTING A PROPOSED BUDGET

Setting up a budget is going to be the most important – and maybe the scariest – process for directors of a new nonprofit organization. However, there must be a budget in place to obtain tax-exemption status. You may also be asked to present your budget when you apply for a private sector or government grants.

The first step is to form a budget committee and defines a deadline to complete the budget plan. If the board of directors is small, they may be involved in budget planning, especially during the organization's first year. Not forming a realistic budget is the main reason that more than half of all new nonprofits fail. Start with the small details and move forward – trying to look at the big picture before figuring out the details almost never works.

Begin by estimating where the revenue coming into the organization is going to come from for the first year, including any grants you may receive. If you are going to include grants in your budget plans, you need to consider whether your organization will meet those grants' requirements and what kind of auditing paperwork you will need to maintain if you're awarded the grant.

Find out if there are restrictions on how the grant funds are allowed to be used. Sometimes, large grants can actually be harmful to the organization because small donors will feel that their money doesn't matter.

You want to seek out grants that will allow the organization to build sustainable programs. If the nonprofit will be offering services to the public for which they can receive funds, consider the expected revenue from those services. For example, some nonprofit hospitals will charge the patient and their insurance company, or nonprofit learning institutions can charge tuition.

Also, nonprofits that will offer a thrift store for the public. Another source of revenue might come from individuals who want to participate in the mission who are willing to offer donations.

Consider seeking government grants that your nonprofit qualifies for. Again, it's important to understand what that revenue is allowed to be used for and what kind of documentation you must maintain if that is where you expect to gain revenue. With limited resources, looking for programs that will allow funds to be used for building a sustainable program will be your best option.

You may also choose to accept funds from private, family, and corporate foundations. Research if there are sources of revenue that align with your nonprofit's mission. Some employers may allow employees to donate portions of their paychecks to your organization.

Once you've determined all the ways you can acquire revenue, simply add it all up. Underestimating your revenue is better than overestimating. This will ensure that you will operate within your budget, meet goals you've set, and even have funds in case of emergencies. The first year will be difficult to estimate because you have no reliable donors or history on which to base your budget.

The budget isn't only determining where revenue will come from, but also how it's going to be spent. Direct costs are one area that nearly all organizations need to spend money on. This can include costs to pay extra staff during fundraising events, money for marketing materials, or other supplies needed for operation.

Consider if you will need to spend money on capital expenses, such as a vehicle for use by nonprofit employees or real estate where the organization can carry out certain functions. A large part of an organization's expenses come from basic operational overhead. This includes salaries or wages for employees and their benefit packages, and monthly bills such as rent, postage, and internet or phone bills.

For a new nonprofit organization, budgeting can be its biggest chore. Seek help from others who have successfully established a non-profit before. Also, IRS Form 990 is a necessary requirement for filling out a budget as well as a great resource for helping new organizations to create their budgets.

Budgeting Tips

• Read all the budget information before you begin calculating your budget.

• If budget forms are provided, use them. Fill the budget forms out exactly as requested.

• Don't get creative with your budget.

• Ask for what you need to do what you have proposed in your application.

• Be as accurate in your budget figures as possible but do remember they are just an estimate.

• Don't include items, like equipment, if the budget guidelines state that funds can't be used for them.

• Make sure your budget matches your objectives and timeline.

• Make sure the numbers in your budget are added and calculated correctly.

• Ensure the numbers you have can be read easily

• Keep copies of the information and numbers used in the budget. Also write down who provided them and how budget figures were determined.

• Have the person who will keep track of how the money is spent work on the budget also.

Checklist for Budget Preparation

• Budget: In a clear way, enlist all costs the funding source is supposed to cater for and those that other parties need to provide.

• The checklist should be similar to the proposal narrative

• Is as detailed as possible

• Should incorporate the items being requested by the funding source

• It should incorporate all the elements other sources will pay

• Includes all volunteers

• Details fringe benefits, separate from salaries

• Includes all consultants

• Separately details all non-personnel expenses

• Includes indirect expenses where appropriate

• Increasing Your Competitive Edge —Helpful Reminder Hints

• Be alert to all sources of funding

• When you receive an application kit, read it thoroughly and carefully.

• Understand the evaluation criteria and address them.

• Fulfill all requirements of the application. Make certain you explain fully how your proposal addresses the priorities.

• If you need ANY clarification, do not hesitate to call the contact named.

• ALWAYS keep your application under the page limit.

• Do not load up the proposal with extraneous information or attachments. Be as DIRECT as possible. Let your narrative tell the full story.

• If you plan to have the project become self-supporting after your project period ends, make that clear in your application and how you intend to do it.

• A well-designed index to your proposal is helpful for reviewers. Designate the pages in the application where required   information can be located.

• Do not use fancy packaging. This is costly and adds no 'brownie points".

• Obtain and include support letters from State and local groups.

• Fulfill all announcement requirements. If clearances are required by the State or other jurisdictions, assure that your package includes these.

• Be certain that your application is sent to the correct address by the deadline date.

• Follow up to make sure the application was received by the specified deadline.

• ALWAYS keep up-to-date spreadsheet logs for every Funder you contact and proposal you submit. This will save you from excessive of confusion later.

ACCEPTED OR DECLINED?

If Your Application is Declined

If your application is declined, first and foremost, don't give up! Many grantors will send you a letter giving you a reason why the grant was declined, and if not, you can always call and ask them for ways to improve your program, service, or grant proposal for next time.

A declined grant is not the end of the world. It is important to keep on applying. Some grantors like to wait until an organization has a little history with grants they've received – they want to see how you utilized the money, and how your organization works to be a sustainable one.

If your grant is declined, don't reapply to the same grantor right away. Wait for a two to three grant cycles to apply again, and by all means, never send them the same application you sent previously. Draft a new grant proposal explaining all the ways your organization has grown and changed since the prior application, what you've learned, and all its successes. Show them why they would want to grant funds to your organization this time.

Some Tips For You If You Don't Get Funded

• Very carefully read your proposal once again. Try to determine the weak points of your proposal.

• Use your contact person at the foundation or government office as a source of feedback. Ask them why they feel the proposal was turned down. If there is still time before the deadline takes effect, revise the proposal and re-submit. However, do not re-submit if there is a chance the original deadline will be missed.

• Remember that a rejection does not necessarily mean the funder will not fund the proposal in the future.

• Identify another possible funder and rework your proposal to meet that funder's guidelines. Then, send it to them. After all, you have worked very hard preparing your submission, and with a little adjustment, your proposal will interest just the right foundation or agency.

• Take the feedback you have received regarding your proposal, and use it to make the proposal stronger. If your idea is a good one, time spent focusing the concept or re-working the budget is an excellent investment.

• Remember that "no" in the funding world really means "hello." A rejection today can be turned into an introduction for tomorrow.

If Your Application is Accepted

You've Got the Grant!

Kudos to you! Your hard work has paid off, and the company has won a grant. When you're a staff member in your company, you've just started a real job; if you've received a grant, the applicant is likely to have a few more writing jobs for you.

If your application is accepted – breathe a sigh of relief and pat yourself on the back! After the cheering is over, the first thing you want to do is be sure to thank the grantor. Send out a thank you letter from your organization's board of directors. Invite the foundation or giving corporation to visit your Agency to see their dollars at work. Always stay in contact with your funders. A good relationship with them ensures grants in the future and success for your nonprofit organization.

If you haven't decided yet until you applied for a grant, assess immediately whether you want to announce it and thank the grant maker publicly. Receiving the grant means that you have a company worth talking about.

Often the acknowledgment of a successful grant is part of the grant contract. Occasionally, particularly in the case of corporate giving programs, the grant proposal also includes a section on how you can acknowledge the gift of the grantmaker. Grantors may want you to make a permanent sign, announce a grant to the media, or include their name in your organizational literature. Be sure to identify all gifts in the way the donor likes.

When you still have funds to collect, you can use the grant as an opportunity to capture other donors. Announce that the donation has taken you to the halfway point of a $2 million capital campaign, or that it has allowed you to buy a truck, and that you're looking for local funders to help you underwrite other program components.

When your grant is for operations, it may not be newsworthy for the public, but you know how valuable these unregulated funds can be. Share the news with your board and rejoice quickly with the staff. Take the fantastic news and share it with everyone!

MORE GRANT WINNING SECRETS

For the past 3 years; my team and I have been writing grant proposals for existing businesses, nonprofit organizations, and even start-ups. I will be sharing with you some of our key secrets.

1. PROGRAMME:

I. What is the setup?

II. Who are the organizers and what are their accomplishments?

III. What are the selection criteria?

IV. When is the deadline?

2. PERSONALITY:

This includes your passion, skills, vision, values, goals, principles, career, and even habits. Always try to define who you are in clear terms.

I. A man without an IDENTITY is a NONENTITY.

II. You can never write about a man you don't know.

III. Most applications will start by asking about you.

What you say can either make them read through or push your application aside, so be careful.

3. PACKAGING:

Don't lie, but package yourself and your organization in a truthful manner.

4. PREDECESSORS:

The fastest way to the top is being led by someone at the top.

I. Ask your predecessors for a sample copy of their application, if possible.

II. Ask them to proofread your application.

5. PERSISTENCE:

I. Without persistence, you will be defeated even before you start.

II. Never give up at your first trial.

III. Dreams don't work unless you do.

IV. While being persistent, you have to remain positive.

Every organization offering grants have their unique feature as such applicants are required to understand what is required by the organization.

For some grant providers, they request for a physical meeting, where applicants will have to pitch their ideas to a panel or an audience.

Some would request for business plans, feasibility reports, and other documents. While, the likes of TEEP, would make their selection from the filled online applications.

Therefore,

• The first secret worth knowing is to understand the requirement for the grant in which you want to apply, stick to it and others follow suit as thus;

• Be addicted to research: this is key to knowing your industry, market, competitors, and then building your business to make a profit while offering your incredible market value.

• Learn to pitch your ideas: You need to be so familiar with your ideas that you can sell it to any investor. Note: Your idea is as good as your ability to sell it.

• During a pitching session, be ready to answer any question that comes your way with confidence.

The need to soak yourself into your idea cannot be overemphasized, and this is because you are the first to believe in your idea before anyone else does.

IS FREELANCE GRANT WRITING FOR ME?

You could become a freelance grant writer with little or no experience, but you're better off getting at least a few years of solid experience as an employee before you make the leap. Being an employee of a grant writing or consulting firm can be of a great experience because you can work directly with different organizations.

At the same time, you may fear the thought of putting yourself out there as a solo act. Where will I find clients? Can I earn enough as a freelance grant writer? Will a bad experience with a client hurt my reputation?

Such fears are completely normal. We would worry if you had no fears at all. Grant writing is done by human beings, not robots.

With that said, deciding whether to take the freelance grant writing plunge requires you to take an honest look at yourself.

Why? For two reasons, basically. First, we bring our strengths, weaknesses, and personal histories to freelance grant writing. Your personality is one of many variables, potentially affecting your success. Furthermore, your strengths can be a weakness in some situations, just as what may normally be a weakness is a strength in certain cases. Your adaptability may offset your weaknesses or inexperience.

Second, freelance grant writing success depends far more on what you actually do than on your personality, which is basically your internal preference to act a certain way in certain situations. Your personality matters little if you aren't getting business cards made, shaking hands at conferences, or doing what you told a client you would do. Freelance success depends on you taking action persistently and consistently.

However, you do need to informally assess what makes you tick. There is no point in taking the action required to become a freelance grant writer if freelancing will make you miserable.

Here are the areas where we suggest you evaluate yourself:

Your Own Sense of Freedom

In what work situation do you feel the greatest sense of freedom?

Be honest. Some people feel the strongest sense of freedom in jobs where the structure is externally imposed. If this describes you, that's fine. But reconsider whether the freelance route is truly for you.

You may be a better fit for freelancing if you comfortably alternate between working independently and interdependently. Both of us performed well as employees when allowed to work relatively autonomously.

The setting in which you feel the strongest sense of freedom may vary over time. We've also known people who were freelance grant writers for a while, but later went back to being a full-time employee. That's fine too.

Once you leave the grind of showing up at an office five days a week for several hours per day, it's hard for many people to go back to it.

Your Risk Tolerance

There are far riskier businesses to start than a grant writing and consulting business.

Nevertheless, freelance grant writing carries its share of risks. You will go through periods of having too many clients followed by not enough. A client may suddenly drop you without explanation. You may get sick. You may need to say goodbye to a client when they become a hot mess and can't handle any grants they get. The government raises your tax burden. The list is almost endless.

Relying exclusively on full-time employment carries risks, too, such as your work being based on one organization and one income stream.

Decide what type of risk you can live with and go from there.

How You Like To Affiliate with Colleagues

Full-time employment can feel fulfilling when you have friends at work. Perhaps you enjoy the general camaraderie in your department.

Having work friends or enjoying socializing doesn't mean you should avoid freelancing.

But if you have a particularly strong need for this kind of affiliation with others, take a closer look at whether freelancing may be for you. At the least, have a plan for how you will get these needs met if you become a freelance grant writer (co-working spaces may be a good idea).

Your Tolerance for Being Alone

Consider to what extent you will like or even tolerate working alone for extended periods. This may be a case where there is only one way to find out, but give this the honest consideration it requires before you take the plunge.

Your family situation and stage of life

If you are the primary caregiver for children younger than the traditional kindergarten age, be realistic about how much freelance work you can actually do. Even if you have regular babysitting help, assume you will work at least occasional evenings and weekends, even if freelancing is a part-time endeavor. Be realistic about how much you can actually get done with young children in the house, even when they are in the higher elementary grades.

Similar considerations may come into play if you have aging parents, especially if they live with you.

Freelancing could be the best working arrangement of all if living with young children or aging relatives. Or, in your unique situation, it could be the worst possible arrangement.

Assess your situation honestly and accurately. You don't want to render yourself unable to do what you told a client you would do.

Your Target Market

We live in the Cincinnati metropolitan area and close to the Dayton, Ohio, metro area. There are a number of other freelancers in the region. However, unlike some metro areas, no single freelancer or grant writing firm dominates our geographic area.

If there is a freelancer or a firm in your area that has cornered a lot of your local market, this should not discourage you from opening up your shop (being a subcontractor for one of these "big dogs" can be a great way to get experience). You need to plan accordingly, though.

Thanks to technology, your target market can be just about whatever you declare it to be. Many grant consultants, such as Ashley, routinely work with clients based outside their geographic areas.

If you live in a remote rural area, you may have no choice but to land clients based far from your home. If higher education is your niche, there may be only a few colleges and universities close to you, which means you will need to carry out your marketing and networking accordingly.

Clear Vision

Most of those we encounter as freelancers are basically good people who want to do the right thing, even when they're being difficult in some ways.

With that said, you will cross paths with a handful of bad actors. Eventually, you will encounter prospective or actual clients who try to do a "bait and switch," flat-out lie to you, take their sweet time in paying you or try to unilaterally change the terms of your service.

You need to be able to distinguish between a good person having a bad day versus a troubled person who will never change. The good news is the chronically, inherently difficult people are relatively few in numbers. The bad news is you will encounter them. As a result of their actions, they will occupy a lot of real estate in your head if you take them on as clients or, if already a client, you continue to associate with them.

Having a clear vision also applies to cases where you like the organization's work, you like their people. Still, they just are not a realistic candidate for getting and handling grants for any host of reasons – weak or no infrastructure, extreme dysfunction, little or no ability to sustain a program or to measure outcomes, and so on.

It's not fun to tell organizations they must address numerous issues before you can help them get grants. But you will have to do so at some point.

Your Ability to Tactfully Take No Garbage

Clients, even good clients, will sometimes make unreasonable demands. Some prospective clients will want you to work for a song.

A client may be chronically uncooperative with your requests for information.

Across scenarios, you need to be able to hold your ground while successfully maintaining the relationship, if there is one.

When you are in your twilight years and looking back on your career, the odds are high you will regret not having done it

If you think someday, you'll look back on your career and say, "Yeah, maybe I should have given the freelance thing a try, but I had a good career and am pretty happy with how it went," that's different than a gnawing, almost unexplainable feeling that you may really regret passing on being your own boss, being a writer, or whatever else about it has deeply moved you to contemplate this.

This one is kind of hard to put into words. You will just kind of know which category fits you here.

Summing It All Up

Some of you who conduct our recommended self-evaluation will fare well. In which case, it's probably a slam dunk, and you should start a freelance grant writing business. For others, your self-evaluation results will be a mixed bag.

Whether you should proceed with freelancing will depend on where you might have an issue.

If you're too "nice," you can learn to be more assertive. If you think working from home for more than a few hours at a time would drive you crazy, well… that's kind of an inherent preference.

No matter the specific outcome of your self-evaluation, we think you will know deep down whether this is right for you and whether you truly want to do it.

REFINING YOUR PLAN AND FINISHING YOUR APPLICATION

Note that your approach is going to grow and change as you go into the grant writing process. Completing your submission without changing your development strategies or altering your priorities usually means that your plan will be strengthened. Establishing a peer review program is an ideal way to find problems with both the reasoning and the writing itself.

Overall, the detection of any weak ties ensures that they will be resolved until the grant program officer reviews the submission. One important way to ensure that your grant application is centered and impact-driven are to define how your initiative can deliver a return on investment. Remember to keep a focus on:

- It's a direct return on investment. Prove that the initiative can hit a quantifiable performance level, such as a measurable engagement level.

- The community's return on investment. Explain the less concrete and important, as well as beneficial effects that your initiative would have on your society.

Another main approach to make the grant writing plan versatile is to cultivate feedback from key stakeholders. Which kind of projects do your supporters, sponsors, voters, and leaders think will be ideal for your company to undertake?

The organization's leaders will also need to accept the final plan, so why not encourage them to provide input and suggestions during the writing process? They might easily identify the weaknesses or opportunities that your organization may have overlooked.

Your team may address the grant writing process in a variety of ways. Grant drafting teams designate different parts of the proposal to specific individuals and submit it in an online document. This encourages the staff to set up an effective editing procedure, so you can quickly guarantee that each segment is reviewed both individually and in the sense of the sections before and after it.

Keep a keen eye for spelling and grammar mistakes, poor words, and unacceptable arguments. When done, ensure that the whole grant application is reviewed several times. When the team is happy with the submission and the nonprofit leader signs it, then it's time to send it back! It depends on the grant source, you may submit your application either electronically or by mail — just make sure to check well in advance.

Remember, the company is part of a community — including other nonprofit organizations. When any nonprofit wins a grant, note that the money is always going to benefit the society in many ways. You may have other funding options, whether through a range of scholarships, online donations, or through other fundraising platforms.

At times, reaching out to the funding authority is a good idea. Calling, writing, or meeting with the grant program officer may be a great idea to explain the alignment of your ideas and the priorities of the granting authority but never communicate to the grant officer plainly just to leave an impression.

Must Be Considered in Grant Proposals

A grant proposal is a very straightforward, concise text sent to a particular institution or funding body with the intention of persuading the recipients to provide you with funds because: (1) you have a significant and fully-considered strategy to advance a worthy cause, and (2) you are accountable and willing to carry out the plan.

When you continue organizing and writing your grant application, ask yourself the following:

Audience

When considering your audience, you will think about the kind of details that these readers would find most compelling. Were they testimonials? Recommendations from other colleagues? Historical precedent? Consider carefully about how you're constructing your point in response to your audience.

What are the Particular Expectations for this Grant?

Pay attention to everything that the granting institution expects of you. Your plan will meet exactly with these criteria. If you receive advice that contradicts the standards of your situation (including from this website), please disregard it! Review the representative samples of popular proposals in your field or proposals that have won a particular grant that you are applying for

How are You Going to Build Your Credibility?

Make sure you show yourself as smart, competent, and thinking ahead. Establish your reputation by the thoroughness of your strategy, the deliberate manner in which you communicate its significance and meaning, and the experience that you have of what's been learned or studied. Please refer to any previous successes that will validate your desire to excel and your dedication to this project. Identify any relationships you have formed with complementary organizations and individuals.

How Can You Clearly and Logically Present Your Plan?

Make sure the organization is rational. Divide the plan into predictable parts and mark it with simple headings. Follow the headings and material criteria set out in the call for proposals of the funding agency.

The proposals for grants are straightforward. It's not an excellent time for you to add your prose with tons of metaphor/twist in literary allusion. The vocabulary needs to be uncluttered and precise. Only use ideas and vocabulary that your readers are familiar with.

Your readers don't have to work hard to grasp what you're talking about. However, use a vivid picture, a persuasive anecdote, or a memorable expression when it conveys the significance or importance of what you are proposing to do.

HOW TO AVOID FINANCIAL SCANDALS WHEN HANDLING MONEY FOR YOUR NONPROFIT

Almost everyone at some point has felt the feeling of disappointment when listening to the news and hearing about yet another nonprofit scandal. The good news is that this does not have to be your story.

There are plenty of successful organizations that have been able to operate and enjoy good reputations while remaining above reproach. You can as well! Let's talk about some concepts that will assist you in avoiding financial scandals when handling money for your nonprofit.

Profit doesn't belong to you. If you can embrace this concept, you will be able to avoid a lot of misfortune as it relates to your 501c3 nonprofit. Although, nonprofits can be profitable - the profit does not belong to you. For example, if you offer inexpensive private tutoring services targeted at low-income families and still end up with $50,000 remaining, that "profit" does not belong to you. You would need to reinvest those funds into furthering the charitable purpose of the nonprofit.

For example, instead of paying yourself the $50,000 outright by writing yourself a check, you could instead propose that the board of directors increase your salary by $50,000 for the following year. This would work if the new increased salary amount would be considered "reasonable compensation."

Don't Abuse Tax Incentives. As a 501c3 tax-exempt nonprofit organization, you will have the luxury of being exempt from federal taxes when making purchases. If you want to avoid financial scandals, you will need to make sure you are not abusing those tax incentives.

Example: Justin wanted to host a launch party for his new tech company. He realized that his funds were low after having spent most of his budget on computers, servers, and equipment for the business. Instead of reducing the budget or waiting to have the event when he could afford it, he decided to wrongfully use his tax-exempt certificate to buy everything for his party. This allowed him to save money by not having to pay sales taxes on any of the decorations, equipment rental, catering costs, venue fees, etc. Since the launch party was not related to his exempt purposes, he is now in violation of federal law.

The same rule applies as it relates to letting other people use your nonprofit's tax-exempt certificate to make purchases that are unrelated to your charity's mission.

Avoid Excess Benefit. Generally speaking, the Excess Benefit Transaction rule means that you shouldn't pay someone unreasonably more compensation than they deserve for the work they've done. In order to avoid violating this rule, I will explain the steps you should take to research and make sure a proposed salary is reasonable based on I.R.S. recommendations.

Three Primary Ways Fraud Occurs in Nonprofits

In addition to the three concepts I just shared, here are three primary ways that fraud occurs in nonprofits:

1. Embezzlement - Someone within the organization will go to a new bank and open an entirely new bank account in the nonprofit's name. They will then deposit are sent to the nonprofit in that account, withdraw the funds and use the money for their own purposes.

2. Fraud - Someone will create a fake company that pretends to be a legitimate vendor of the nonprofit. They will provide fake invoices to the nonprofit and pay for fake services to the fake company.

3. Misappropriation of Funds - Someone with access will use the nonprofit's debit card for personal purchases.

Now that you know the ways fraud commonly occurs in nonprofits, here are also a few things you can do to reduce the likelihood of financial scandals in your nonprofit:

Background checks - require that anyone that works for your nonprofit pass a background check. This will help you know if prospective employees have a criminal record or a history of fraud.

Check references - Before you hire someone or allow them to get involved with your nonprofit, request references, and call the references to inquire as to the person's character.

Check cash in the account - You should make it a habit of monitoring cash flows in your nonprofit's bank account regularly so that you can immediately report any suspicious activity.

Pay attention to vendors - When reviewing the bank account ledger, if you see any suspicious vendors that were paid from the charity's account - inquire and make sure they are legitimate.

Accounting Software - Use actual software to monitor financial transactions within your nonprofit so that you can recognize trends and monitor financial activity.

Limit cash - Try not to accept cash to the best of your ability. Instead, try to process payments via debit or credit cards since electronic payments are easier to track

Financial Controls - Require that checks are signed by multiple people within your charity for accountability purposes.

Lock up checks - Do not leave the nonprofit's checkbook out in the open as an easy target for theft.

Check work during vacations - Encourage your staff and employees to go on vacations. When they are out of the office, take this opportunity to check their desk, computer, email, and any electronic records they may have. Make sure you have provided them with an email policy in advance to let them know that emails are the property of the company and that they should not assume any expectation of privacy when using company equipment or devices.

Be honest - Don't embellish accomplishments of your nonprofit or overstate expenses.

Segregate duties - Make sure different members of your staff are handling different financial tasks within your charity so that there is accountability and no one person has complete access to everything. Your CPA or accountant can help you with properly dividing up the roles.

Dissolution - If you decided to shut down your nonprofit, make sure that all assets (cash, equipment, property, etc.) are transferred to another tax-exempt nonprofit per the I.R.S. Code instead of going into the wallets of a board member or stakeholder.

What are Financial Statements

Your nonprofit is accepting donations and spending money toward your mission. Instead of having to spend hours poring over hundreds or thousands of individual transactions (purchases and deposits) on the bank statements of your nonprofit account and doing the math to reach conclusions, you should generate financial statements for the nonprofit.

Financial statements are scorecards that let you view the health of a nonprofit by looking at a summary of its transactions or activities on a few pages. They are far less cumbersome than having to review hundreds of receipts and pages of bank statements. Financial statements are generated using a commonly accepted set of accounting principles or rules that allow nonprofit founders, board members, banks, and funding organizations to compare nonprofits from different industries in a universal way.

Financial statements are similar to sheet music for musicians. They allow people that are unfamiliar with a song, or in this case, your nonprofit, to read the sheet music (financial statements) and immediately understand the music (the health of your nonprofit).

Why Financial Statements are Important

Even though, you are keeping your own records and tracking numbers for your nonprofit, it may be a good idea to generate financial statements on a regular basis.

Financial statements can help your nonprofit in the following ways:

1. Know the health of your nonprofit. Financial statements allow you to easily track many of the numbers that are important to know if your nonprofit is healthy and growing.

2. Know if your nonprofit is in the "black." Financial statements will allow you to see all of your expenses and your income on one page (typically). This will let you know immediately if you are making money or losing money in your nonprofit. For example, you will be able to see if the donations you receive from events are more than the donations you receive from online campaigns, etc. You can also tell if you're spending too much on staff, programming, or if you need to increase the budget in those areas.

3. Allows Others to Understand Your Nonprofit. In the future, you may decide that you would like to apply for grants or apply for a bank loan. In each of these scenarios, you will likely need to have financial statements prepared for your nonprofit so that the other parties (lenders, funding sources, etc.) can assess the financial health of your organization.

3 Types of Financial Statements

There are three (3) primary types of financial statements: Income Statement (also known as the Profit & Loss Statement), Balance Sheet and Statement of Cash Flows. It would take an entire book to discuss how powerful each of these financial statements is and explain all of the ways that they can benefit your nonprofit. However, here is a brief overview of each statement:

1. Income Statement / Profit & Loss Statement (P&L) – On the most basic level, the Income Statement tells you how much money your nonprofit brought in and the bills the nonprofit had during a certain period of time. In order to make money in a nonprofit, you will need to have money left over after you pay all of your bills. This is a basic definition of "profit". The P&L lets you see the "bottom line" or your profit or loss after everything was paid during a specific time period (month, quarter, year, etc.) Here are just a few things an income statement will tell you about your nonprofit:

- How well is your nonprofit performing?
- Is your nonprofit profitable (making money after the bills are paid)?
- Are you over budget or paying too much in some areas?

2. Balance Sheet – The Balance Sheet lets you see your assets (things you own) and your liabilities (what you owe others) at any given moment in your nonprofit. Examples of assets would be cash in your bank account, all equipment your nonprofit owns, and accounts receivable (money other people owe you). Examples of liabilities would be credit card debt, and loans and wages owed to employees. Here are just a few of the things a balance sheet will let you know about your nonprofit:

- If you need more cash reserves (money saved)
- If you can handle more debt
- If you can handle growing or expanding
- If you need to be more aggressive with collecting money owed to you

3. Statement of Cash Flows – To put it simply, a Statement of Cash Flows tells you where your money is coming from and how it is being spent during a period of time. Some nonprofits are profitable but go out of business because they did not have enough "cash on hand" to pay their bills. This can happen if the timing of when your bills are due and when you get paid is not aligned. Your Statement of Cash Flows can help you see if this is or will be a problem and correct it in advance.

WRAPPING UP

While there were many important points discussed in this book, I hope you remember the following:

Make Goals

Regardless of what phase you are in your nonprofit, remember to make actionable and measurable goals. Have your team give input in making these goals and make sure everyone understands the goals the organization is currently pursuing.

When you are successful in achieving a goal, celebrate, and then make more challenging goals. You should always push to achieve new he

Keep Detailed Records and Processes

Keep detailed records of everything your organization does and fails at. This helps with forming repeatable processes. It should be easy for anyone new in the organization to see what efforts were made in the past, how successful they were, and what didn't work.

Eliminate Waste

As a nonprofit, it is imperative that you operate as cost efficient as possible. Do not waste funds on unnecessary services and products. This also holds true for your time. Do not waste your time on tasks or volunteers that are not beneficial to the organization.

Be Creative

One of the biggest determining factors in how successful your nonprofit will be is how creative you are in solving the problems placed in front of you. Be creative in how you attempt to raise funds, attract volunteers, run programs, and advertise what you are doing. As a nonprofit, you will always be strapped for cash. Do not always try to solve your problems with money. Instead, look for ways to get what you need without spending cash.

Remember This Is Business

People often mistakenly think of a nonprofit as something different than a business. Your nonprofit is a business! You should run it as such. You should run it as such. Negotiate with people, provide quality service, and always present yourself professionally.

I wish you lots of success in running your nonprofit. I hope this book prevented you from many of the common pitfalls of starting a successful nonprofit, and provided you with valuable tips and resources.

CONCLUSION

Grant writing has a great ability to help the nonprofit organization to achieve its goal. A grant that funds a significant new initiative will mark the beginning of a new development period for the nonprofit company and draw expanded interest and potential supporters. Yet, it takes time and energy to write and submit grant applications.

Attempting to apply for grants is tough work, and many come with conditions attached, such as parameters for the allocation of funds. Besides, you may be up against a number of other eligible groups for available resources. It means that your institution must have a clear vision and a smart operating foundation. Grant-giving agencies do not fund a nonprofit that they don't believe would last. Prove to them that yours is here to last with the firm backing of non-grant sources as well.

The process of developing a grant proposal can be one heck of a task. People think of grant writing as a linear process when, in fact, it is a circular process that starts with an idea. The secret to developing a winning grant proposal is to clearly describe the specific problem you intend to address before you can actually proceed into designing a program that will address it. Then, you can move on to giving a detailed description of the funding source.

If it is the very first attempt for your nonprofit organization, the whole process eventually benefits the organization, whether you get the grant or not! The main goal for you is to eventually have a well-conceived proposal that gives a properly laid out strategy that addresses the problem at hand and clinch the funds to pay for it!

Many grant programs aren't popular, and thus, don't receive many applications from the public. This may be because the government doesn't do the best job marketing and/or because the application process is intimidating.

That shouldn't hold you back! You now have the scoop on where to look and even how to have NOFOs emailed to you. You know where to sign up, and you have an idea of what you'll encounter along the way.

Spend some time considering how your organization can serve the needs of the public. I'd also recommend that you occasionally search the Grants.gov website to see what NOFOs are out there; that may cause some ideas to pop into your mind.

There are lots of programs that may inspire you to try something new or give you an idea of how you can meet a public need that you didn't know existed.

Whatever you do, you have to bear in mind that a strong grant proposal cannot be developed in a single day. This means that you have to start the whole process pretty early so that you have ample time to get feedback from reviewers reading your draft. Seek out a wide range of readers from specialists in your area of research to non-specialists (layman).

So, now you have all the tools you need to write a grant for a nonprofit organization. No doubt you are feeling a little overwhelmed, however, think of writing the grant as if you are having a meal of several courses – take the time to savor and digest each course (each part of the grant application) before moving on to the next. Make sure your boilerplate is complete, and you can use it as a guide for each type of application you make.

Best of luck and happy grant-seeking!

Made in United States
Troutdale, OR
04/21/2025

30797100R00046